CHOPIN

Piano Sonata

No. 2 in B-flat Minor
Opus 35

Sonate.

F. CHOPIN. Op. 35.

11744

42

come sopra.

11744

Scherzo.

48

50

11744

Marche funèbre.
Lento.

F. CHOPIN. Op. 35.

52

11744

Presto.

sotto voce e legato.

56

*) Between measures 8 and 9 are found, in earlier editions, *two measures more* which Chopin crossed out with his own hand in the copies belonging to Princess Czartoryska and Frau Streicher.

11744

Printed in Great Britain
by Amazon

45320985R00015